Red is the Royal Blood

by Tshiama Nambombe

iUniverse, Inc.
New York Bloomington

Red is the Royal Blood

iUniverse books may be ordered through booksellers or by contacting:

iUniverse
1663 Liberty Drive
Bloomington, IN 47403
www.iuniverse.com
1-800-Authors (1-800-288-4677)

ISBN: 978-1-4401-3009-0 (pbk)
ISBN: 978-1-4401-3011-3 (cloth)
ISBN: 978-1-4401-3010-6 (ebk)

Printed in the United States of America

iUniverse rev. date: 03/23/2009

Dedication

To all my teachers from Doncaster University Centre, particularly Jean Granville, who helped me a lot for the realization of this book, my friends, especially my best friend Maria Namubiru, who also was very useful during the manuscript preparation. Thank you for helping to make my dreams come true.

And to all my family and my children, who are continuing to make me proud.

Preface

This play originated as an exercise for the Bachelor of Arts [Honours] Scriptwriting curriculum, at the University Centre, Doncaster.

After many revisions and rewrites, the present script was produced.

The play in three acts, takes place in a mythical African country, and the themes covered are resonant with concerns in contemporary society; themes such as tradition, power, class, and civil order. The characters are well defined, displaying human frailties such as greed, envy, lust, and of course love.

Thus by the act of performance audiences may reflect upon the human condition.

It has been a pleasure to work on this project by Tshiama Nambombe and in this age of instant electronic entertainment engaging in live theatre is to be applauded and encouraged.

Jean Graville-King,

Social Science Lecturer

Doncaster University Centre

Casting

Ne-Nsundi: The King

Ne-Bondo: The prince, king's brother

Ne-Makaya: The princess, king's daughter

Ne-Basilua: The Queen mother, king's mother

Ne-Mpungi: Justice civil servant

Mwe Mbuku: Foreign affairs civil servant, then commander in chief of the army.

Ne-Nsaku: Commander in chief of the army

Ndungi: Kingdom's shaman

Mavadidi: The sculptor

Besadi: First Notable

Other Notables
Messengers, Farmers, peasants, dancers…

Prologue

[When the curtains open, a man dressed in multicolored linen plays tom-tom. Then two storytellers appear. They wear cloths made from "macout" a local term meaning fabric made from straw.]

STORYTELLER 1: In the middle of the sixteenth century, the ancient kingdom of Kongo is at its political high point. Ne-Nsundi, the king, rules with equity and impartiality.

STORYTELLER 2: Ne-Nsundi allows his subjects to participate in some decisions after debates have taken place.

STORYTELLER 2: The activities of the royal court are supported by an expansive system of civil servants. And the most fearsome is Ne-Nsaku. He brings misery to villagers through extortion, bribery, and assassinations.

STORYTELLER 1: This period was characterized by a love triangle, jealousy, hate, and treason, which resulted in rebellion and an incursion by enemy armies.

STORYTELLER 2: The fact that Mavadidi, a sculptor, loves the princess, Ne-Makaya, does not please Ne-Nsaku, the commander in chief of the army. Mavadidi is his sworn enemy because Ne-Nsaku loves the princess and wants to marry her. Officially, royal blood cannot be mixed. But don't forget one thing: red is the royal blood.

ACT I

Scene 1

[Palace Courtyard. A dance is taking place around objects representative of Nzambi A Mpungu Tulendo(1). Dancers are dressed in multicolored linens: the men are covered up to their hips, and the women are covered up to their breasts. In the middle is the man playing tom-tom.]

Scene 2

[Mavadidi's Workshop. Different traditional objects are displayed on the wall. Mavadidi dresses in plain linens fixed securely around his waist. He's sculpting Ne-Makaya's face. Ne-Makaya sits on a well-adorned throne and is dressed in a long, multicolored tunic that extends from her neck to her ankles.]

MAVADIDI: Princess—or shall I call you wife—today, I am shaping your face, which will be admired from generation to generation as proof of my infinite love.

NE-MAKAYA: I will be your wife from eternity to eternity.

MAVADIDI: Will your father allow it? Can you convince him?

NE-MAKAYA: My father is an understanding man. He wants me to be happy. The only unpredictable reactions will be from his Notables. They're very conservative.

I'll be breaking taboo and tradition by marrying a sculptor.

MAVADIDI: That's why I am wondering about those conservative men who are stuck on the word *tradition*.

NE-MAKAYA:	We will face a hard opposition, but we must not give up. Prejudice and gossip of the kingdom will never separate us.
MAVADIDI:	The power and strength of our love will outlast all those against it.
NE-MAKAYA:	In two weeks, my father, his Notables, and his civil servants will come and visit your workshop. Show him my sculpture. I am sure it will please him. Then tell him of your feelings for me.
MAVADIDI:	Under no circumstances will I allow anyone to destroy our love. It has only grown after what we have been through together.
	[Mavadidi finishes the sculpture and hands it to the princess.]
NE-MAKAYA:	What a marvelous work!
	[The princess puts the sculpture on the floor and embraces Mavadidi.]
	It's splendid! I have never received such a gift in my life. I will take my sculpture to the royal palace, where my father will admire it night and day, and my ancestors' spirits will lead my mother to come and contemplate this wonderful sculpture.

[Mavadidi takes Ne-Makaya's right hand.]

MAVADIDI: It's time for you to go. You know that at this time, you must help your grandmother.

Scene 3

[**Royal Palace. In every corner are set wooden Kongo sculptures with nails—nkisi nkondi(2), or the power figures. It is the dwelling place of an ancestral spirit and used by Kongo divinity. Behind the king hangs a Kongo ivory trumpet with a carving of a royal figure. King Ne-Nsundi sits on a well-adorned throne. He wears a long, multicolored tunic that covers him from neck to ankles. Near him sits his brother, Prince Ne-Bondo, who also wears a long tunic, but his is different from the king's. On either side of the throne sit Notables, each dressed in a piece of cloth tied firmly around the waist and falling above the knee. Another piece of cloth is tied across the chest and the back.**]

NE-NSUNDI: Gentlemen, I welcome you. Some time ago, our kingdom knew trouble. We lost our valuable civil servants during the war against our neighbors. The reason for your presence here today is to receive confirmation of your appointment. Ne-Mpungi.

[Ne-Mpungi stands.]

Today, you shall have responsibility for justice in the kingdom. You will judge and condemn culprits and acquit

	innocents with proof and evidence. Be righteous and equitable. Are you ready to be committed?
NE-MPUNGI:	Yes, your Majesty, I am.
NE-NSUNDI:	Ne-Nsaku.

[Ne-Nsaku stands.]

I appoint you commander in chief of the army. Your task is to deter all future rebel incursions in our kingdom. Are you able to take this new responsibility to the point of giving your own life?

NE-NSAKU:	Yes, your Majesty, I am. I promise to be faithful to you and the kingdom.
NE-NSUNDI:	Mwe Mbuku.

[Mwe Mbuku stands.]

I appoint you to be in charge of foreign affairs. Are you ready to respect the code of good neighborhood and be respectful of our guests?

MWE MBUKU:	Your Majesty, I am.
NE-NSUNDI:	**[Taking his sword and touching the shoulders of each in turn.]**

On the fourteenth day of January 1555, I declare you civil servants.

Scene 4

[Forest of Loanga. A peasant and his adult son and daughter are making palm wine. Ne-Nsaku, wearing a multicolored tunic, arrives with his men.]

NE-NSAKU: (arrogantly) Peasant, my men informed me you have not yet paid your tax for protection.

PEASANT: My Lord, I do not have money at the moment. This year's palm trees did not give good wine. Next month, I shall pay twice the amount.

NE-NSAKU: (roaring with laughter and looking at his men) Did you hear that? Tell this peasant how much Nzimbu (3) is owed to the commander in chief when someone fails to make a payment.

ALL: Four.

NE-NSAKU: Did you hear that, peasant?

PEASANT: Yes, my Lord. I—

NE-NSAKU: We will keep your daughter as collateral.

PEASANT: No, my Lord. Please have pity!

NE-NSAKU: Tell me, peasant. Is she betrothed to anyone?

19

PEASANT:	Yes, my Lord. She is betrothed to Kiabelua's son.
NE-NSAKU:	Kiabelua's son? The crook young man? **(to his men)** Take the girl.
PEASANT:	Mercy, my Lord. She is of much help since her mother died.
	[One of Ne-Nsaku's men grabs the girl and holds her. The peasant kneels.]
	Spare my daughter, my Lord. I shall pay four times.
NE-NSAKU:	Good. Release her.
	[Ne-Nsaku and his men leave.]

Scene 5

[Royal Palace. King Ne-Nsundi,
Prince Ne-Bondo, Queen Mother
Ne-Basilua, and Princess Ne-Makaya
sit on the floor, dressed in long
tunics like before. Similar pieces
of cloth extend across their chests.
They are assisting in a traditional rite
performed by Ndungi, the shaman or
Nganga(4), who is dressed in raffia.
He holds a wand and casts a spell.]

NDUNGI: Get out from here! Let Nzambi A
Mpungu Tulendo protect the one who
reigns among us with justice and equity.
Get out from here malevolent spirits
that bring darkness. Let Nzambi A
Mpungu Tulendo protect our king and
his family.

[He kneels by the king.]

Your Majesty, you are the greatest king
on earth. Your kingdom is the largest,
most powerful, and most beautiful in
Africa. You take care of your subjects.
You treat them with kindness. When
you give a feast for the principal men
of the capital who come to visit, you
regale them with the best millet bread,
much meat, and abundant mwamba
(5). Our ancestors sent me to grant you
force and strength to rule this kingdom.
Your reign will last years and years. No
malevolent spirits will be able to destroy

21

you. Nzambi A Mpungu Tulendo will protect you. The great way is not the work of men; it is Nzambi A Mpungu Tulendo

NE-NSUNDI: Ndungi, you've all my confidence. From generation to generation, your family has been loyal. In misfortune and in happiness, you always take care of us. Our gods bless you, too.

NDUNGI: Majesty! Nzambi A Mpungu Tulendo sees all and rules all. His will is always done. He gave us basic laws and traditions. It is his law and his absolute wisdom that underlay the oaths and rituals of loyalty.

NE-BONDO: We can't go against his wishes, Ndungi. We owe him reverence and respect.

NDUNGI: Majesty! This morning, some of your Notables will try to oppose your desire, but Nzambi A Mpungu Tulendo will always be with you.

NE-NSUNDI: Nzambi A Mpungu Tulendo deserves our devotion. **(to Ne-Basilua and Ne-Makaya)** Ladies, Notables' Council will soon start.

[Ne-Nsundi, Ne-Basilua, and Ne-Makaya exit. Ne-Bondo and Ndungi remain in the royal palace.]

Scene 6

Morning. Tom-tom sounds announce the beginning of elders' council. Enter Mwe Mbuku, Ne-Mpungi, and others Notables and civil servants. Ne-Nsaku is the last to enter. The Notables are dressed in multicolored cloths that cover them from the hips to the feet. Some minutes later, Ne-Nsundi enters with two guards. Ne-Mpungi claps his hands.]

NE-MPUNGI: Gentleman, King Ne-Nsundi. All stand.

[Ndungi holds a traditional sculpture figurine from Mboma(6), moves slowly to the king's throne, and starts the incantation.]

NDUNGI: Oh, Majesty! You are the protector of our kingdom against malevolent forces. You are the protector of our wives and our children. Without you, no life exists. We are here to honor your greatness. You provide the light and the rain that sprinkle on our harvests. Be blessed by our gods and our ancestors. We are here to glorify you. We are—

NE-NSAKU: **(interrupting)** Oh, you, shut up and stop this humbug.

NDUNGI: Humbug? What are you talking about?

NE-NSAKU:	I am talking about your nonsense. His majesty does not need your flattery. Do you forget your role? You are here to predict the future and, especially, to tell us when our enemies will attack. Of course, *you* have only bad omens. And another thing, in this kingdom, Nzambi A Mpungu Tulendo is our God. We have to glorify only on his name.
NDUNGI:	Does your rank of dignitary give you the right to defy the ancestors and the established order?
NE-NSAKU:	Established order? Established order! I am neither defying ancestors nor established order. Do you want to cast a spell on me? Who was the last person you put a spell on? It was Matondo's husband. Why? Because you desired his wife. Funny, isn't it? Poor little man. Now he cannot walk anymore. Nor can he perform in the marital bed.
	[The Notables are amused by this. Ndungi turns on them.]
NDUNGI:	Sacrilege! There is a sacred, natural power of nature. There is the political power of domination. And there is power that comes from our ancestors and tradition. The second is derived from the third, and this leads to permanent order. Transforming these powers just for innovation will lead to

	disorder. Honorable Ne-Nsaku has to respect order.
NE-NSAKU:	Philosophy! Always philosophy!
NDUNGI:	Insane person.
NE-NSAKU:	No, I am not insane. You are insane.
NDUNGI:	How dare you insult the protector of all spirits? Tell us about your concubines. To carry out some superstition, one of them sacrificed her baby. Do you remember? She strangled him and buried the body in the nkenge (7) cassava field. She thought this act would increase her fertility. Ridiculous, isn't it?
NOTABLES:	Ridiculous. This is ridiculous.
NDUNGI:	You came and asked me for assistance. I gave you idols to protect you, your concubines, and your house. Shall I continue?
NE-NSAKU:	Rubbish. I did no such thing.
NDUNGI:	Rubbish? I know many secrets in this kingdom.
NOTABLES:	Oh! Oh! Oh!
NDUNGI:	No one can challenge me.

MWE MBUKU: Have you no shame you two? It is
               dishonorable to wrangle in front of his
               majesty. Today is the tenth anniversary
               since our queen passed away. We are
               obligated to respect her memory. **(to
               Ne-Nsundi)** Majesty, forgive us for this
               misunderstanding.

NE-NSUNDI: Our concern today is to seal our alliance
               with the Mani Soyo (8). But our spies
               tell us the chief of Mani Soyo is trying
               to help the rebels.

MWE-MBUKU: What can we do your Majesty?

NDUNGI: **[Raising the wand in his right hand
               and statue in his left, he steps toward
               the Notables.]**

               Have we lost faith in our gods?

NE-NSAKU: Always with a wand and statue in your
               hands. What are you going to do with
               them? I command the armed forces
               of this kingdom. Our soldiers are
               sufficiently equipped to fight any army.

NE-BONDO: Silence! What is the matter with you
               two? What kind of rivalry is this?
               We should be discussing the current
               problems. We should consider the
               interest of the kingdom. Your arguments
               are pathetic.

MWE MBUKU:	Majesty! We apologize for this argument.
NE-NSUNDI:	Dear compatriots. Today is the tenth anniversary of the death of our royal highness. We cannot forget her because she did many good works in the country. But today we have another priority; so there is no official ceremony for the queen. The situation is serious. Our kingdom is threatened by rebels. Their swords are more powerful than ours. Times are bad, and quarrels between us will only destroy the kingdom. We must extend our sovereignty, annexing rebellious provinces. We are, and remain, the powerful kingdom in Africa. The villagers must contribute and make some effort. Now! **(to Ne-Nsaku)** Will you explain your plan to us?
NE-NSAKU:	**[Standing, carrying the map.]**
	Thank you very much, your Majesty. I will recruit all males between the ages of fourteen and forty.
NE-NSUNDI:	Honorable Ne-Nsaku. Fourteen years? Is that not too young?
NE-MPUNGI:	Your Majesty, I shall suggest sixteen years old.
NE-NSUNDI:	What is your suggestion Ne-Bondo?

NE-BONDO:	Sixteen years old is a reasonable age. I agree with honorable Ne-Mpungi.
NE-NSUNDI:	Mwe Mbuku?
MWE MBUKU:	I agree as well.
NE-NSUNDI:	Honorable Ne-Nsaku, go on.
NE-NSAKU:	At the moment, a smaller corps of heavy infantry is necessary. I will expect soldiers to have two weeks worth of food upon reporting for campaign duty.

[**Opening the map.**]

We will take position from north to south and west to east. We will defeat them. We must encircle the enemy on all corners.

MWE MBUKU:	Is that all?
NE-NSAKU:	What do you mean?
MWE MBUKU:	Your plan is unclear. We know your position; however, you do not tell us how you will proceed.
NE-MPUNGI:	We need a consistent plan. Otherwise—
NE-NSAKU:	(**interrupting**) I know their position. In order to raise support against our enemies, we have to make concessions to others.

28

MWE MBUKU:	Are you sure?
NE-NSAKU:	Of course. To prevent the kingdom from falling into the hands of Soyo and its allies, we must follow my plan.
	[Notables murmur.]
NE-NSUNDI:	Alright. **(to Ne-Nsaku)** I hope that your plan will work; otherwise, we will all be reduced to slavery. Dispatch a spy to see what is happening on our borders. Send our emissary to contact our future allies. Your plan must be explained in depth.
NE-NSAKU:	Yes, your Majesty. I will go at once.
NE-NSUNDI:	**(to Notables and elders)** Next week, we will start the second period of slashing and-burning fields in Mpyaza(9). It will be the beginning of the thirteenth month. This date is marked by the death of Mbenza, the initiator of our painting workshop. To honor him, we will make our annual visit to appreciate the talent of our artists. Thank you gentlemen for your presence. See you in the next council.
	[Exit King Ne-Nsundi and prince Ne-Bondo. All Notables bow and kneel.]

Scene 7

[**Mavadidi's Workshop. Various
sculptures are exposed. Ne-Nsundi,
Ne-Bondo, Ne-Makaya, Mwe Mbuku,
Ne-Nsaku, Ne-Mpungi, and other
Notables enter. While admiring the
works by Mavadidi, they see the
princess Ne-Makaya's sculpture.**]

NOTABLES:

(**the Notables are stunned, except Ne-Nsaku**) Oh! Oh! Oh!

NE-BONDO:

What beautiful work!

NE-NSUNDI:

[**Caresses the face of the sculpture.**]

It is, indeed. (**to the princess**) My
daughter! Have you seen the way you
have been honored by Mavadidi?

NE-MAKAYA:

Yes, Father. It's wonderful!

[**Ne-Nsaku looks dejectedly at the
princess.**]

NE-NSUNDI:

Mavadidi, your sculpture displays a rare
emotion and beauty. This is something
magical and wonderful. Everything is
sacred. In my life, I have never thought a
work of art could be as splendid as that.
It seems you have brought a paradise to
Nsundi Kingdom.

MAVADIDI: Your Majesty, it's an honor that you
              recognize the value of my work. I am
              an artist. I work with wood and clay,
              but only artistic eyes such as your's can
              understand the beauty of the work.
              A sculptor can see his dream come to
              reality in his art.

              [Kneeling.]

              Your Majesty, you gave me the freedom
              to realise my art. I am thankful to you.

NE-NSUNDI: Please stand, Mavadidi. I must thank
              you for furthering the greatness of our
              kingdom. People may die, generations
              may be overtaken, but your art can
              never be destroyed. The glory of our
              kingdom will be sung; stories will be
              told from generation to generation.
              Artist, tell me: How can I reward you?
              What gift can I give you?

MAVADIDI: Majesty, your appreciation is the best
              thing I can receive from you. An artist
              does not need material gifts but the
              recognition of his work.

NE-NSUNDI: Mavadidi, I truly appreciate your art,
              and I wish to reward you as proof of my
              gratitude. If I do not reward, how can I
              convince myself that I appreciated your
              work?

MAVADIDI:	Majesty, I cannot answer. My inspiration has come from you. It's only you who can grant me. Majesty! If I ask you for something precious, will you grant it to me?
NE-NSUNDI:	I will give you anything you want, Mavadidi.
MAVADIDI:	Majesty, I am in love.
NE-NSUNDI:	Are you? Tell me, who is this woman? Since I am your king, I can give you whatever you want. Who is she? My guard will be ready to bring her for you immediately.
MAVADIDI:	Majesty! I would give all my soul and my body to her. I have never stopped loving her.
NE-NSUNDI:	Tell me who is she?
MAVADIDI:	**[After a brief hesitation, Mavadidi looks at Ne-Makaya.]** Princess Ne-Makaya. Your daughter is the one I— **[Ne-Makaya feigns astonishment.]**
NE-NSAKU:	**(interrupting)** Sacrilege! Blasphemy! Profanity! This is an offence against your Majesty. He deserves the death sentence for this.

NE-MAKAYA:	Death sentence? Are you serious? Who are you to pronounce a death sentence? Why does a man in love deserve this kind of penalty?
NE-NSAKU:	You are a mere girl, and as such, you have no right to speak in front of elders and Notables of the kingdom.
NE-MAKAYA:	Mere girl? A girl who can provide seed, do all those things that a woman can, carry out at home, and satisfy a husband? It is a long time since I was a mere girl. I am a woman now. The choice belongs to me and me alone.
NE-NSAKU:	Do you know why the queen mother, your grandmother, did not come here? Because she knows that her place is not among men.
NE-MAKAYA:	Really? Do you usually ask questions and give answers yourself? Are you God, making decisions in the place of others? As for my grandmother, she belongs to the old class that believes women have no rights.
NE-NSAKU:	With all due respect, your highness, the rules concerning women's silence in front of men are strict. Mavadidi deserves death.

MAVADIDI:	Death sentence? His majesty said he could give me whatever I ask. Does someone deserve a death sentence because his heart feels love for another?
NE-NSAKU:	Shut up, Mavadidi. Do you assume you own the world because you are a good artist?
NE-BONDO:	Notable Ne-Nsaku, you should avoid confrontation with others. This often causes enemies.
NE-NSAKU:	What are you talking about?
NE-BONDO:	Do you not remember your last confrontation? Ndungi did not appreciate your words.
MAVADIDI:	Do you know why the mouth is first to rot after death? Because it talks a lot of nonsense.
NE-NSAKU:	Mavadidi, you should turn your tongue a thousand times before speaking. It will be better for everybody.
NE-NSUNDI:	**(interrupting)** Enough. **(to Mavadidi)** I have heard your request. A decision will be made in the next council session.
MAVADIDI:	Yes, your Majesty. Your decisions are incontestable.

NE-NSAKU: Majesty, lions and sheep never drink
                 water from the same pond.

NE-NSUNDI: Notable! Keep your thoughts to yourself
                 for now. The council will decide: either
                 Mavadidi will or will not be authorized
                 to marry princess Ne-Makaya.

MAVADIDI: Thank you, your Majesty.

NE-NSUNDI: Now let us leave Mavadidi to continue
                 his extraordinary work.

                 [Exit the king, Notables, and guards.]

Scene 8

[Forest of Loango. Mavadidi and the princess sit on the branch of tree.]

NE-MAKAYA: Day and night I pray to Nzambi A Mpungu Tulendo, asking him to withdraw any Notable opposition.

MAVADIDI: What can we do if there is any?

NE-MAKAYA: We can fight. We'll fight until the end of our lives. Neither my father, nor my uncle, nor my grandmother, nor any Notables will be able to take away what I feel for you.

MAVADIDI: My love for you is endless. I'll take it to the tomb. You are, and will forever be, my love.

NE-MAKAYA: You are kind and honest.

[They hear something moving.]

Did you hear that?

MAVADIDI: Yes. What do you think it is?

NE-MAKAYA: It's very strange. We should go now. This forest is full of rebels and bad spirits.

MAVADIDI: Then let us leave.

CURTAIN

ACT II

Scene 1

[Ne-Nsaku's House. All walls are adorned with animal skins, expressing his talent as a hunter. He sits on a well-decorated chair. His wife enters, kneels, and puts down a bowl full of groundnut and corn.]

NE-NSAKU: Good. A woman must look after her husband.

MATONDO: I must satisfy all my dear husband's wishes.

[One of Ne-Nsaku's men enters. He's out of breath. Ne-Nsaku claps his hands, and his wife exits.]

NE-NSAKU: Speak. What happened to you?

THE MAN: We saw the princess in the forest with Mavadidi.

NE-NSAKU: Sacrilege! The Notables have not made their decision yet!
What were they doing?

THE MAN: Talking.

NE-NSAKU: Talking? About what?

THE MAN: We are not sure.

NE-NSAKU:	**(embarrassed).** Foolishness! We must have something to tell the king.
THE MAN:	Oh! Yes, they were seen engaging in a sexual act.
NE-NSAKU:	Much better.

Scene 2

[Royal Palace. Same set. Late night. Ne-Nsundi sits with Ne-Basilua.]

NE-NSUNDI: Mother, during our visit to Mavadidi's studio, he expressed his desire to marry Ne-Makaya as a reward for his work.

NE-BASILUA: What did you tell him?

NE-NSUNDI: That the Notables' council will make the decision. If they say yes, he will marry my daughter. If they say no, I shall not be able to do anything for him.

NE-BASILUA: My son, you are the king. You can make a decision without consulting the Notables. After all, it's about the life of your own daughter.

NE-NSUNDI: Mother, I must listen to the people.

[Ne-Nsaku enters. Ne-Basilua exits.]

NE-NSUNDI: Sit, Ne-Nsaku.

[Ne-Nsaku sits.]

NE-NSUNDI: What brings you at such a late hour?

NE-NSAKU: I have news regarding Mavadidi and the princess. They were together in the forest.

NE-NSUNDI: Continue.

NE-NSAKU: They were seen being intimate, your Majesty.

NE-NSUNDI: Are you sure of what you're saying?

NE-NSAKU: Yes, your Majesty.

NE-NSUNDI: And you saw it yourself?

NE-NSAKU: No, your Majesty. One of my men—

NE-NSUNDI: I want witnesses. Good night.

Scene 3

[Royal Palace. King Ne-Nsundi sits on his ornate throne. Ne-Makaya enters.]

NE-MAKAYA: Hello, Father. Your servant said you wish to see me.

NE-NSUNDI: Yes, indeed.

NE-MAKAYA: It is late. Can it not wait until tomorrow?

NE-NSUNDI: It is about you and the artist. People have seen you alone with him in the forest.

NE-MAKAYA: **(disappointed)** Your men have been spying on me?

NE-NSUNDI: I am your father. It is my duty to take care of you.

NE-MAKAYA: I am not a foolish girl.

NE-NSUNDI: You are the princess. You have to be careful.

NE-MAKAYA: I am a virgin, and I shall remain so until the day of my marriage. Do you not trust me?

NE-NSUNDI: I do trust you, but you must use caution.

NE-MAKAYA:	I'm going to bed. Good night, Father.
NE-NSUNDI:	Good night.

Scene 4

[**Royal Palace. The royal throne is up center. Some Notables and elders stand in the corner of the council room.**]

NE-NSAKU: Have you ever heard of such a thing! An artist wants to marry the princess. How can we mix blood? It's sacrilege! Can we really accept such a thing?

NOTABLES: (**ad lib**) Oh no! We can't let it happen.

NE-NSAKU: We have to fight for the nobility. We must stop this kind of insanity.

NOTABLES: (**ad lib**) Yes, we must. This is unacceptable.

[**Ne-Nsundi enters, and the room falls quiet.**]

NE-MPUNGI: Gentlemen, King Ne-Nsundi. All kneel!

[**Ne-Nsundi sits on his throne. Near him sits Ne-Bondo. All Notables, elders, civil servants, and Ndungi take their places.**]

NE-NSUNDI: Notables, elders, and wise men of the kingdom, a week ago we promised to answer Mavadidi concerning his request to marry the princess. Our judgment must be just and without prejudice.

I ask Prince Na-Bondo to make the statement on the situation.

NE-BONDO: This case is complex. A subject of a different class wishes to marry the princess. During this debate, I want everyone to be guided by his heart. Whatever grievance you may have against Mavadidi, I ask you to be objective. Ne-Mpungi, the assembly wishes to hear you now.

NE-MPUNGI: Your Majesty, Notables, and constituent members of the assembly, after admiring the extraordinary beauty of Mavadidi's work, the king asked him what gift he desired. Mavadidi expressed his love for Ne-Makaya. Our wise majesty promised him an answer from this meeting. Be it positive or negative, the reasons will have to be explained to him.

NE-BONDO: Ne-Nsaku, the council will hear you.

NE-NSAKU: Your Majesty and Notables, let us not let this man deride our traditions. It is an offense to fall in love with a virgin princess. Royal blood cannot be mixed with common blood. And you—

MWE MBUKU: (interrupting) Why not? Red is the royal blood.

NE-NSAKU: Yes, but it is sacred. Do you want to allow this artist to taint royal blood? We

MWE MBUKU:	cannot amend the ancestral law. Honourable Ne-Nsaku. You have never accepted the established order. Why now?
NE-MPUNGI:	May I remind you of the origin of the Kongo Kingdom? In the beginning, the highest positions were occupied by artists. They are the founders of our kingdom.
NE-NSUNDI:	Enough! This is not the place for fighting. **(to Ne-Mpungi)** Move on.
NE-MPUNGI:	Tonight, we must answer several questions: First, does an artist have the right to marry a princess? If yes, then should we abolish our tradition? Second, do we have the right to condemn someone to death simply because for falling in love with a princess? Notables, I appeal to your integrity of judgment. No one should be influenced by another. And everyone is free to express his thoughts. After this discussion, we will proceed to a secret vote. I have spoken.
NE-NSAKU:	Your Majesty, Notables, and elders, as I said earlier, a man of inferior social class can never marry a princess. Such a union will bring misfortune to our kingdom. Indeed, many elders and sages are in agreement with me on this point.
NE-MPUNGI:	Ne-Nsaku, you may speak only for

	yourself.
NE-NSAKU:	My apologies. We should not just say yes because it is expedient. Saying yes will not only abolish our tradition regarding blood mixture, it will also affect other traditions. Traditions established generations ago and that work well. This case is no reason to replace them. Why should we apply clemency for a person who has violated our sacred laws and principles?
MWE MBUKU:	Tradition is not law, Ne-Nsaku.
NE-BONDO:	**(interrupting)** Since these discussions began, I have stayed quiet. All of you have heard what Ne-Nsaku said. But consider this: the man we are considering executing emerged from his mother's womb. Imagine his mother's pain when she hears that her son was executed because he loved a woman? The daughters of dignitaries are women first. They have the maternal instinct, and they, too, will feel pain. None of you would allow *his* son to suffer such a fate. Sentencing this man to death will be the greatest crime the kingdom could commit. I have spoken.
NE-NSAKU:	The question is not whether this man came from the womb of a woman. We should not regard him as a victim. The law applies to everyone. If we cannot condemn him because he fell in love with the princess, then we must

condemn him for disrespecting the king. Our laws are clear about such an act. He deserves death. I have spoken.

NOTABLE 1: If we condemn this man, the young will revolt. If we offer clemency, the young people will take it as an example of leniency. So what can we do now?

NOTABLE 2: Executing this man will make him martyr. I believe that life imprisonment would be a better option for everyone.

NOTABLE 3: What woman would accept that her son was sacrificed in the name of an outdated law? Think carefully because a life depends on it. Notables and elders, this man deserves neither death nor jail. Love comes from the heart.

NE-NSAKU: He walks all over our traditions. Such a fault deserves punishment. None other than death. Not only did he express his wish to marry our princess, but he did not wait for the decision of the Notables before engaging in improper acts with the princess.

NOTABLES: (**ad lib**) Oh! It's abominable.

NE-MPUNGI: Have you witnesses, Ne-Nsaku?

NE-NSAKU: Yes.

NE-MPUNGI:	Good. Before any decision is made, let us hear them. Bring the first witness.

[Enter the peasant.]

NE-MPUNGI:	Tell us, sir, what exactly have you seen?
PEASANT:	I saw the artist in the forest with the princess.
NE-MPUNGI:	What were you doing in the forest?
WITNESS 1:	I was checking my palm wine.
NE-MPUNGI:	And when you saw the artist and the princess, what were they doing?
WITNESS 1:	They were in the throes of passion.
NOTABLES:	**(ad lib)** Oh! Outrageous!
NE-MPUNGI:	Sir, is it not true that you are in debt to Ne-Nsaku? How are we to know you are not making this up in hopes of reducing what you owe? You do not have to answer. You may go.

[The peasant exits.]

NE-NSAKU:	How dare you?
NE-MPUNGI:	Notables. We have heard the witness, but there is doubt as to his credibility. Therefore, let us take a moment for reflection. When you return, we will vote.

Scene 5

[Royal Palace. Two guards exit. King
Ne-Nsundi, Prince Ne-Bondo, and
some guards remain. A man plays
tom-tom. A group of dancers enter.
After several minutes, Ne-Bondo claps
his hands to stop the dancers.]

NE-NSUNDI: Thank you very much. You may go.

[Notables and elders reenter. Two
guards follow, bringing Mavadidi.]

NE-MPUNGI: We are now prepared to vote. You will
Each find four small sticks in front
of you. Red is for the death sentence,
black symbolizes life in prison life, blue
is for total acquittal, and yellow is for
neutrality. Without regard for another's
vote, please raise the stick representing
your choice.

[Notables and elders raise their sticks.]

NE-MPUNGI: Four red, one black, one yellow, and
three blue.

[Ne-Mpungi looks toward the king.]

The sentence of death has been chosen.

[Negative murmurs from some of the
Notables.]

NOTABLES:	**(ad lib)** Nonsense. Nonsense.
NE-NSUNDI:	**(to guards)** Put him in jail while he awaits the day of his execution. But first, Mavadidi, do you have anything to say before you go?
MAVAVIDI:	Yes, your Majesty. Why have I been brought here as a thief? I was told I could ask for whatever I wanted. Why should I be shackled thus?
NE-NSUNDI:	The Notable and elders have found that your demand was too excessive. The majority has decided.
MAVADIDI:	That is the Notables' judgement. What is really in your heart, your Majesty? Is falling in love with the princess such an awful offense?
NE-NSUNDI:	Mavadidi, I do not wish for such a fine artist as yourself to die. It's not yet too late. If you agree that you will never see the princess again, your life will be spared.
MAVADIDI:	How can I say that, your Majesty? How can a firefly not be attracted to moonlight? How can a bee survive without a flower? I can never give up my heart's desire. No, your Majesty, I can never betray my heart.

NE-NSAKU:	Mavadidi, you have flouted the royal traditions.
MAVADIDI:	Could you send your own son to death because he has publicly expressed his love? You can't. You can't because you have done all this to defend your own interests. You have bought the voices of others in order to achieve your ends.
NE-NSAKU:	Blasphemy! How dare you. Stop him!
NE-BONDO:	This man is facing the death sentence. He has the right to express what is in his heart.
MAVADIDI:	Your Majesty! I have not flouted the traditions. I have not committed any offense. Princess Ne-Makaya overwhelms my mind. I am an ordinary artist who loves the princess. Love does not recognize classes and differences.
NE-NSAKU:	Shut up, impudent man.
NE-NSUNDI:	Ne-Nsaku, let him express all his thoughts.
MAVADIDI:	I admitted in this court that I love the princess. What kind of justice is death, your Majesty? I am being silenced. Should I not speak the truth? My feelings may be hushed. But can't you hear someone's heart beat?

NE-NSAKU:	Mavadidi, you will be punished for your impudence.
MAVADIDI:	What difference can it make? Alive or dead, I won't renounce my conviction. Royal rules have always slain true love, but love has always won in the end! And in spite of all your powers, you cannot wipe out my love.
NE-NSAKU:	Notables and elders can wipe out your existence. Majesty, this man should be executed before the sunset.
NE-NSUNDI:	Enough! This man will be executed when I order it. Guards, put him in chains.
	[Exit Ne-Nsundi and a few Notables. Ne-Nsaku, Besadi, and a few other Notables remain.]
NE-NSAKU:	The king is losing all reason. His state of mind is not normal. He is weak and making compromises with criminals.
NOTABLES:	**(ad lib)** Yes. That's true.
NE-NSAKU:	Are we going to let him destroy our kingdom?
NOTABLES:	**(ad lib)** Oh no.

NE-NSAKU:	We must take things into our own hands. We must overthrow him, or else one day, our kingdom will fall into the hands of the enemy.
NOTABLES:	**(ad lib)** Yes. We have to overthrow him.
BESADI:	My friend, if anyone denounces us, we shall be exiled.
NE-NSAKU:	Exile? We have the support of more than five provinces. The dukes of those provinces have also pointed out the weakness of the king. If anyone must go to exile, it is Ne-Nsundi.
BESADI:	It is suicide.
NE-NSAKU:	So be it! Who's with me?

[All but Besadi raise their hands.]

Who is against me?

[No one responds.]

As I can see, notable Besadi is neither for me nor against me. No matter. You are all men of my trust. No decision shall be made without your consent.

A NOTABLE:	What is the plan?
NE-NSAKU:	We need Mani Soyo's help. Besadi, will you contact their duke.

BESADI: No. I cannot accept.

NE-NSAKU: All right. Who will volunteer?

[Several Notables raise their hands.]

NE-NSAKU: Thank you for your loyalty.

[Pointing to one of them.]

Thank you. You are loyal, and I am sure you will be successful.

Scene 6

[Royal Palace. Ne-Nsundi sits in an ornate chair. Two guards stand on either side. Ne-Basilua enters. Guards exit.]

NE-BASILUA: Is something troubling you my son? You haven't seemed so sad since Ne-Lunama passed away.

NE-NSUNDI: I'm not sad.

NE-BASILUA: Yes, you are. Do I need to remind you that you were in my womb for nine months? I know every movement, every mood of yours more than anyone else. I've always known when you were lying. One day, when in the company of other Notables' children, the king's musician said you destroyed part of his instrument. When I asked you, you said you didn't. But you could not look me in the eye. I told you, "My son you are lying to me." You asked me how I knew? I told you, "Every mother knows when her children are lying." Now tell me what is going on? Is it about Mavadidi's death sentence?

NE-NSUNDI: Yes mother. Personally, I could not make this kind of decision against Mavadidi. A death sentence against someone who has declared his love is unfair and unreasonable.

NE-BASILUA:	You are the king, my son. You can change this decision.
NE-NSUNDI:	I can't change a council decision.
NE-BASILUA:	Council knows you are the king of Nsundi, and you can make a decision without their consent. Are you afraid of Ne-Nsaku's reaction?
NE-NSUNDI:	No, Mother. Ne-Nsaku wasn't the only one who voted for the death sentence. I have to respect the decision of the council. Mavadidi is a good and brave young man, but he made a big mistake. Our tradition does not allow behavior like that.
NE-BASILUA:	Still, you are the king, and you can revise a Notables decision. Mavadidi does not deserve the death penalty.
	[Enter Princess Ne-Makaya and Ne-Bondo.]
NE-MAKAYA:	Death sentence? So that's why you forbade every woman the right to attend the council? Father! Why did you make this decision? Why did you sentence Mavadidi to death? Was this your decision, or is Ne-Nsaku behind it?
NE-NSUNDI:	Our council decisions are not always unanimous. This was a majority decision. Anything that has been done is

	for your own good.
NE-MAKAYA:	How can they know what is good or bad for me? What about you? You are not only the king, but you are also the guardian of the kingdom and its laws and traditions. You know what is right and what is wrong. How can you accept such a decision? If you had a son and you were any other subject in the kingdom, would you accept that your son was executed because he fell in love?
NE-NSUNDI:	You are a princess, my daughter.
NE-MAKAYA:	I am also a woman. Why do you need Notables to make this kind of decision?
NE-NSUNDI:	I can't make an important decision like this without having the consent of the Notables.
NE-MAKAYA:	Your court does not even give the defendant a chance to defend himself. And I am sure that any witness provided by Ne-Nsaku was bribed. What sort of justice is this?
NE-NSUNDI:	I did it to protect you.
NE-MAKAYA:	Protect me? How can you protect me from an innocent man? Father, Mavadidi does not deserve death. He only expressed what was in his heart. If you want to protect me, you would do better to protect me from Ne-Nsaku.

NE-BASILUA:	Don't speak like that to your father.
NE-MAKAYA:	Some minutes ago, I thought you were against the council decision. But I think you're really on their side.
NE-BASILUA:	Not at all. I am on the side of the truth. I can't accept someone's death simply because he's fallen in love with a princess. But you must speak to your father in a reasonable tone, whatever the fault committed.
NE-MAKAYA:	Ne-Nsaku has considerable influence among the Notables. He can persuade anyone to do what he wants. He became a powerful commander in chief because he was given every privilege. Now everyone is afraid of him. He corrupts everyone?
NE-NSUNDI:	How do you know that?
NE-MAKAYA:	People talk.
NE-NSUNDI:	My beloved daughter, are you in love?
NE-MAKAYA:	Will my answer make you change the council's decision?
NE-NSUNDI:	No, my daughter. I have faith in their decision.
NE-MAKAYA:	I am not talking about Notables. I am

talking about Ne-Nsaku.
[Enter a messenger.]

MESSENGER: Majesty, there is talk of a conspiracy to kidnap the princess.

NE-NSUNDI: Who wants to kidnap the princess?

MESSENGER: Rumour has it that it is one of your Notables.

NE-NSUNDI: Do you know the name of this notable?

MESSENGER: No, your Majesty.

NE-NSUNDI: I cannot reign with presumptions. I need proof.

MESSENGER: There is something else, his Majesty.

NE-NSUNDI: What is it?

MESSENGER: I have been sent by some notables to inform you that there is another conspiracy aiming to assassinate you.

NE-NSUNDI: I shall make a decision later if Notables and elders will be able to meet me. But I can't alert the council because of noise.

[Exit the messenger.]

NE-BONDO: Majesty, you could perhaps consider what the messenger has just said. There is no smoke without fire.

NE-NSUNDI:	We will need to reflect before giving an answer. Be wary of chattering, my brother.
	[A prison guard enters out of breath. He bows.]
NE-NSUNDI:	Guard! What happened?
	[Ne-Nsundi claps his hands; Ne-Basilua and Ne-Makaya exit.]
NE-NSUNDI:	Speak guard.
GUARD:	Your Majesty, a group of insurgents want to kill the artist. Fortunately, all the prison guards stopped them.
NE-NSUNDI:	How many dead?
GUARD:	None, your Majesty.
NE-NSUNDI:	What is going on here?
	[Ne-Mpungi enters. Ne-Nsundi claps his hands. The guard exits.]
NE-NSUNDI:	**(to Ne-Mpungi)** Call the Notables for an urgent council meeting to be held at the royal palace tomorrow before sunset.
	[Exit Ne-Mpungi.]

Scene 7

[Royal Palace. Ne-Nsundi sits on his throne upstage center. Ne-Bondo sits to his right, and Ne-Mpungi sits to his left. Enter Ne-Nsaku, Mwe Mbuku, Ndungi, and all Notables. They sit down stage left and right.]

NE-NSUNDI: Notables and elders, yesterday, a group of people wanted to assassinate Mavadidi in his cell.

NE-NSAKU: Assassinate? Mavadidi is a convict awaiting death. His life is no longer important. Whether killed today or tomorrow, there is no change.

NE-NSUNDI: Fortunately, their plan has failed. The death sentence will be stayed until we have had the opportunity to hear testimony to clarify certain facts.

NE-NSAKU: Clarify?

NE-NSUNDI: The assailants have support. We do not yet know who he is, but we will find out soon.

NE-NSAKU: Support? This is ridiculous.

NE-NSUNDI: Guards. Take Ne-Nsaku outside.

               [A prison guard enters, out of breath.]

NE-NSUNDI:	Guard! What is the problem?
GUARD:	Your Majesty, the prisoner escaped.
NE-NSAKU:	Escaped? I knew this would happen. This is the result of your cowardice. Those who wanted to assassinate him, thought only of accelerating the process.
NE-MPUNGI:	Incorrigible. This can only be your fault.
NE-NSAKU:	My fault! When the crops fail, it is Ne-Nsaku's fault. When somebody has a problem, it is Ne-Nsaku's fault. Of course, I'm not Agriculture or Social minister. I am the commander in chief of the army.
	[Ne-Nsundi whispers to Ne-Mpungi.]
NE-MPUNGI:	This council is suspended. We have just learned the dead body of Notable Besadi was found in the woods. Let Nzambi A Mpungu Tulendo keep his soul. We will reconvene in seven days.
	[All Notables exit. Ne-Mpungi and Ne-Bondo stay.]
NE-NSUNDI:	Ne-Bondo, it is your responsibility to organize Besadi's funeral.
NE-BONDO:	Yes, your Majesty.

NE-NSUNDI: Ne-Mpungi, the Notables' council must know what really happened. Keep an eye on Ne-Nsaku.

NE-MPUNGI: Yes, your Majesty.

Scene 8

[Royal Palace. Ne-Nsundi sits on his throne, Mwe Mbuku, Ne-Mpungi, and Ne-Bondo are nearby. Ne-Makaya enters and bows.]

NE-NSUNDI: What is it?

NE-MAKAYA: My father, I have something to tell you. It's of the highest importance for the future of the kingdom. I heard everything that was said in the council.

NE-NSUNDI: I have no doubt, my daughter. I know you very well.

NE-MAKAYA: Many people have told me that Ne-Nsaku instigated the conspiracy. I also have evidence that he bribed other Notables to obtain the death sentence for Mavadidi.

NE-NSUNDI: Who are these people?

NE-MAKAYA: Villagers. They are farmers who have had enough of being robbed by Ne-Nsaku's men. Those brave people are suffering. They are paying a lot of taxes.

NE-NSUNDI: Will they testify before the council of elders?

NE-MAKAYA: I think they fear reprisal, but some of them would like to speak to you.

MWE MBUKU:	I always knew Ne-Nsaku was hiding something. It was strange the zeal he used to obtain Mavadidi's death sentence. We were really fooled.
NE-NSUNDI:	We have not been fooled, but we did have confidence in one of our Notables. I want to see all elders and Notables now. We must discuss this matter.

[Mwe Mbuku exits.]

(to the princess) Thank you very much, my daughter. Go to your grandmother. She has something to explain to you.

[Ne-Makaya exits. The sound of tom-toms is heard calling the elders and Notables. Ne-Nsundi, Ne-Bondo, and Ne-Mpungi mime talking. Mwe Mbuku, Ndungi, and some Notables and elders enter one by one. Ne-Nsaku is the last to enter. All Notables look toward him.]

NDUNGI:	O, king! Dispenser of the wisdom of the ancestors! We are here to listen to your advice. You always tell the truth. With you, injustice does not exist.
NE-MPUNGI:	Everyone knows now the way Ne-Nsaku intimidates people.
NE-NSAKU:	I don't know what you are talking about.
MWE MBUKU:	About your tricks.

NE-BONDO: Today's meeting is your concern.

NE-NSAKU: The person judged is Mavadidi. He escaped from the royal prison.

NE-NSUNDI: Ne-Mpungi, read for us the list of crimes of the accused.

[Ne-Mpungi stands before the Notables.]

NE-MPUNGI: On this date of March, fifteen hundred thirty-nine, the royal court of Nsundi has noted the following abuses committed by the Notable Ne-Nsaku, commander in chief of the army. First, to reinforce his wealth, Ne-Nsaku did charge the farmers excessive taxes.

NE-NSAKU: Rubbish.

NE-MPUNGI: Second, the notable Besadi died under mysterious circumstances, and the court thinks that you are the prime suspect.

NE-NSAKU: Simple presumption. You have no evidence.

NE-MPUNGI: Third, to satisfy his selfishness, Ne-Nsaku has bribed certain Notables so they would vote for the death of the artist Mavadidi, and so eliminate his rival.

NE-NSAKU: Rival? Who's rival?

NE-MPUNGI:	Four, Ne-Nsaku sent to death our fighters in the front line.
NE-NSAKU:	Your Majesty, I protest. This text is completely ridiculous.
NE-NSUDI:	Ridiculous? That is the only word you have in your mouth.
NE-NSAKU:	You don't have any evidence.
NE-MPUNGI:	Enter the first witness.
	[The guard enters with Farmer 1.]
NE-NSAKU:	Farmers! Nonsense.
NE-MPUNGI:	**[Points to Ne-Nsaku.]**
	Do you know this man?
FARMER 1:	Yes, my lord.
NE-MPUNGI:	The court wants to hear your evidence.
	[Farmer 1 hesitates.]
NE-NSUDI:	Speak, farmer. Do not fear. You are under royal protection.
FARMER 1:	Ne-Nsaku's men took more than two thousand Nzimbu shells, which I had saved.
NE-MPUNGI:	Second witness, please!

[The guard enters with Farmer 2.]

NE-MPUNGI: **[Points to Ne-Nsaku.]**

Do you know this man?

FARMER 2:   Yes, my lord. His men killed my daughter's fiancé because Lord Ne-Nsaku wanted her.

NE-NSAKU: Ridiculous. How dare you farmers say this?

NE-MPUNGI: Enter the third farmer.

[The guard enters with Farmer 3.]

FARMER 3:   He destroyed all my harvest because I refused to join the assailants who planned to murder Mavadidi.

NE-MPUNGI: Mavadidi, you can enter now.

[Ne-Nsundi beckons Mavadidi in.]

NE-NSAKU: (surprised) Mavadidi?

NE-NSUNDI: Yes. He is.

NE-NSAKU: I protest most strongly your Majesty.

NE-NSUNDI: As king, it's my responsibility to protect my subjects, especially when they are in danger. Mavadidi had been hidden following my instructions.

NE-NSAKU:	Majesty—
NE-MPUNGI:	(**interrupting**) Mavadidi, the court wants to hear now your explanation.
MAVADIDI:	Your Majesty, Notables, and elders, I can prove Ne-Nsaku used flawed evidence to obtain my death sentence. He secretly loved Princess Ne-Makaya, so he wanted me to be killed. It was the only way for him to satisfy his desire.
NE-NSAKU:	What do you mean? What are you talking about?
MAVADIDI:	Notable Mwanza is an eyewitness of Ne-Nsaku's tricks. Mwanza refused to be corrupted, so Ne-Nsaku threatened to kill him.
NE-MPUNGI:	Mavadidi, in the name of King Ne-Nsundi and the court, accept our apologies.
NE-NSUNDI:	Approach Mavadidi.
	[Mavadidi approaches the king.]
NE-NSUNDI:	In a few days, the royal family will set the day of your engagement to Princess Ne-Makaya.
NE-NSAKU:	Blasphemy! This kingdom cannot go against tradition.

NDUNGI:	This is your end, Ne-Nsaku. You are a finished man.
NE-NSAKU:	Shut up charlatan.
NE-NSUNDI:	Guards! Take Ne-Nsaku away. **(to Ne-Nsaku)** This is the beginning of your exile.
	[Guards exit with Ne-Nsaku.]
	(to Mavadidi) There is someone waiting for you in the Royal room.
MAVADIDI:	Thank you, your Majesty.
NE-NSUNDI:	Servant, take Mavadidi to the princess.

CURTAIN

ACT III

Scene 1

[Royal Palace. While the curtain is closed, tom-tom drums announce an emergency situation. Women and children scream, and the sound of the rebels' violas and trumpets are heard. When the curtains open, Ne-Nsundi, Ne-Bondo, and Ne-Mpungi sit in their respective places. The messenger enters and kneels in the front of the king.]

NE-NSUNDI: Messenger! What is happening?

MESSENGER: Ne-Nsaku and the Mani Soyo troops are attacking.

NE-NSUNDI: Where are they?

MESSENGER: They are at the border. There are three thousand warriors armed with bows and arrows

NE-NSUNDI: What else?

MESSENGER: Some of our soldiers have been captured.

NE-NSUNDI: Tell the new commander in chief to come see me.

MESSENGER: He's on his way, Majesty. He knows the situation.

[The messenger exits.]

NE-NSUNDI: The men, women, and children of the kingdom know that since my crowning, I have always been protected against the peculiarities of people such as Ne-Nsaku. He used looting, extortion, and murder to strike fear in the heart of the populace. And now he wants to destroy our kingdom? As long as Nzambi A Mpungu Tulendo is with us, he won't be able to do it.

[Ne-Basilua enters.]

NE-BASILUA: What's wrong, my son?

NE-NSUNDI: Ne-Nsaku and his soldiers are attacking the kingdom.

NE-BASILUA: Are there any casualties?

NE-NSUNDI: We don't know yet, but some of our soldiers and farmers have been captured.

[Ndungi and Mwe Mbuku enter.]

NE-NSUNDI: Please sit. Our kingdom is being attacked by the Mani Soyo, led by Ne-Nsaku. Mwe-Mbuku, can you handle it?

MWE MBUKU: Yes, your Majesty. Soldiers are en route. I will join them soon.

NE-NSUNDI: If I had known Ne-Nsaku's intentions, I wouldn't have spared his life.

NDUNGI: Man is ordered by wisdom to examine his personal attitude. It was difficult to understand how a man like Ne-Nsaku wanted to conquer the kingdom. The best thing you did was not sentence him to death. This shows your great wisdom. Sentencing him to death would have made him a martyr. And some of our citizens would have venerated him as a god.

NE-NSUNDI: I approve your wise words, Ndungi. Facing this treason, we are determining how to conquer our invaders and push them back. The superiority of our army will annihilate Ne-Nsaku and his allies.

MWE MBUKU: I already sent our soldiers, Majesty. I promise to send a second group if the situation becomes worse. But if the first group is able to push Ne-Nsaku out of Nsundi, we will capture him.

NE-NSUNDI: Good. I have every confidence in you.

[Mwe Mbuku and Ndungi exit.]

NE-BONDO: Majesty, I will join the army to push back Ne-Nsaku.

NE-NSUNDI:	No, my brother, I need you here. I have confidence in Mwe Mbuku. Everything will be all right. In this troubled time, we must reinforce our relations with Portugal because we need some weapons to fight our enemies.
NE-BONDO:	Mwe Mbuku can't forget that Portugal will not help without a price.
NDUNGI:	They are trying to convert us to their religion. But we have our Nzambi A Mpungu Tulendo, and we don't need to change.
NE-NSUNDI:	What do you think, Ne-Mpungi?
NE-MPUNGI:	The best idea is to wait for the visit of the emissary.
NE-NSUNDI:	What is your plan, Ne-Bondo?
NE-BONDO:	I am planning to establish diplomatic relations with some African kingdoms and European countries. We will talk about all of this when the Portuguese king's emissary comes. Even if we must pay the price, we need their help.

Scene 2

[Ne-Makaya room. Ne-Basilua is seated on the ground. Princess Ne-Makaya arrives, accompanied by two female slaves. She sits to the queen mother's right. Ne-Basilua claps her hands, and the slaves leave.]

NE-BASILUA:
I am the grandmother of the Nkumba-nkumba line. When we left Kinlaza, we had only five caravans—five men of royal blood. To help them exercise their duties with peace and dignity, they were anointed with the bones of our dead ancestors. The way was clear. There was no hatred, except for the family of Ne-Nsaku, who created disturbances. I am your grandmother. A clan's mother cannot refuse the marriage of her granddaughter whatever the origin of the young man proposing.

NE-MAKAYA:
I know, Grandmother. You are the wise one. I'm sorry for accusing you and Father of being on Ne-Nsaku's side. I understand that you never realized what he was doing

NE-BASILUA:
We are all of the same blood. Your father understands that Ne-Nsaku's ambition blinds him to the truth.

NE-MAKAYA:	Yes, Grandmother. But now everything has worked out well. Grandmother, tell me about boys and girls when you were growing up.
NE-BASILUA:	From early infancy to the age of five or six, boys and girls were subject to the dominant influence of their mothers. From her they learned the fundamental restrictions; to her they owed their apprenticeship in the language and knowledge of family history. They also learned to imitate her gestures, to recognize foods in their natural state, to observe the boundaries that delineated places and actions that were prohibited.
NE-MAKAYA:	My marriage is going to be celebrated soon. It is necessary for me to learn to be a mother.
NE-BASILUA:	Yes, indeed! Next is the period of separation. The girls slept in the house of the women; the boys slept in the house of the men. The dividing line between the sexes destroyed the integrity of the family unit formed by the mother and her young children. Very quickly, boys discovered their superiority and the advantages of the masculine condition: apprenticeship, hunting, fishing, handling agriculture equipment, initiation in the recognition of plants and their uses, and assistance at the Notables' councils. All the rights we

	women can't have.
NE-MAKAYA:	And the girls?
NE-BASILUA:	The girls continued their education at their mothers' side. They prepared themselves to become skillful in domestic tasks and the work of the fields; the girls gradually learned the role of the wife. Girls had to give very early proof of their talents to attract the attention of young men. Mavadidi saw all kinds of those qualities in you. That's why he wants to marry you. But before we could marry, girls were subject to—

[The messenger enters.]

NE-BASILUA:	What is the problem? What brings you here?
MESSENGER:	Did you hear the tom-tom?
NE-BASILUA:	No.
MESSENGER:	The king wants you to be somewhere safe.
NE-BASILUA:	What?
MESSENGER:	Queen Mother, I have to take you somewhere safe.
NE-MAKAYA:	What is this about?
MESSENGER:	It's a matter of kingdom security.

NE-BASILUA: I am the Queen Mother. Tell me what is going on.

MESSENGER: With all due respect, Queen Mother, I can't.

[The messenger, Ne-Basilua, and Ne-Makaya exit.]

Scene 3

[**Palace Courtyard. Offstage is heard the sound of tom-toms and a distant crowd shouting. On stage is the palace, Ne-Nsundi sits on his throne. Near him sit Ne-Mpungi, Ndungi, and other Notables and civil servants.**]

PEOPLE: Ne-Nsaku is dead. Long live King Ne-Nsundi! Long live Prince Ne-Bondo! Long live Princess Ne-Makaya! Long live the Queen Mother! Long live Mavadidi!

NE-NSUNDI: Ne-Nsaku is dead. The rebels have been defeated. Everything is back to order. We had no difficulty in annexing Mpangu, Nkusu, and Wandu. The governors of those provinces came willingly and without resistance. In spite of their earlier resistance, the provinces of Nsundi and Mbamba and all rebel provinces have been annexed. From today, the following royal leaders are named: Prince Ne-Bondo is the representative for foreign and social affairs, while Mwe Mbuku is our new commander in chief, having coped so well in his interim role during the war against the rebels. Mwe Mbuku, what say you.

MWE MBUKU:	After the war and the death of Ne-Nsaku, our army has to be restructured. We must eradicate all corruption, such as was introduced by Ne-Nsaku and his men. Every recruit will be trained before going to fight.

[People continue cheering.]

PEOPLE:	Ne-Nsaku is dead. Long live King Ne-Nsundi! Long live Prince Ne-Bondo! Long live Princess Ne-Makaya! Long live the Queen Mother! Long live Mavadidi!

Epilogue

STORYTELLER 1:   Do you hear that? Long life for the royal family! Long life for the artist!

STORYTELLER 2:   It is sure that Ne-Nsaku died. But Ne-Nsaku has many descendants. Will they easily forget the death of their father, or will they seek revenge?

STORYTELLER 1:   The next part of life in Kongo Kingdom holds the answers.

CURTAIN

(1) Nzambi A Mpungu Tulendo: God in the Kingdom of Kongo
(2) Nkisi Nkondi: Fetishes sculpture
(3) Nzimbu: Currency
(4) Nganga (Shaman): Protector of the kingdom's traditions
(5) Mwamba: Peanut butter
(6) Mboma: One of the clan
(7) Nkenge: One of the fields
(8) Mani Soyo: one of the rival's Kingdom
(9) Mpyaza: Cold season in Kongo kingdom